N R⊕E S

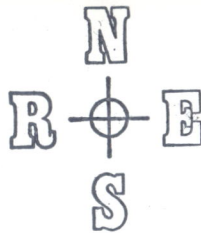

THE WESTHILL PROJECT R.E. 5–16

MUSLIMS

2

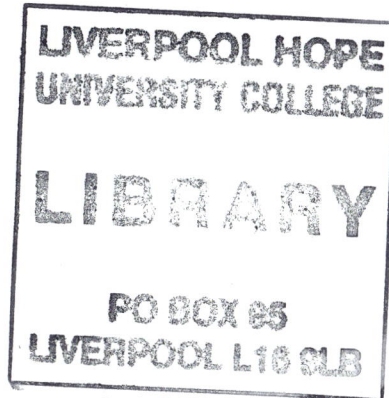

GARTH READ
JOHN RUDGE

Muslim consultants

Rashida Sharif

Ghulam Mustafa Draper

M·G·P

MARY GLASGOW PUBLICATIONS

Published by Mary Glasgow Publications Limited,
Avenue House, 131–133 Holland Park Avenue,
London W11 4UT.

Typeset in Great Britain by Anneset,
Weston-super-Mare
Printed in Great Britain by W S Cowell Ltd,
Ipswich

British Library Cataloguing in Publication Data

Read, Garth
  Muslims.
  2
  1. Islam — For schools
  I. Title II. Rudge, John III. Series
  297
  ISBN 1–85234–074–6

Acknowledgements

The authors and publishers are grateful to the following for permission to use copyright material:

Photographs

Cover:
Jerry Wooldridge
Peter Sanders (couple cutting cake)

Inside pages:
Jerry Wooldridge pages 7, 8, 9, 10, 11, 12, 13, 19, 20, 21, 23, 35, 36, 37 (bottom), 38, 40, 42, 43, 44, 51, 58
Peter Sanders pages 29, 30, 31;
Margaret Breiner page 37 (top).

Text

English translations of passages from the Qur'an are taken from the text with notes by S. Abul A'la Mandudi, English rendering by Muhammad Akbar Muradpuri and 'Abdul 'Aziz Kamal, published in 1987 by Islamic Publications (PVT) Limited, Lahore.

The illustrations on pages 5, 6, 15, 16, 17 and 18 are by Gerry Woods, on pages 22, 24, 25, 26, 27 and 28 by Lorna Turpin, on pages 33, 34, and 61–3 by Maggie Brand with calligraphy on pages 62–3 by Abdullateef Whiteman, on pages 45, 46, 47, 48, 50, 53, 54, 55, 56 and 57 by Hemesh Alles and on page 49 by Ian Foulis.

Contents

1 Muslim Community Life

Messages

Have you ever played a game of passing messages from person to person? Somebody makes up a message and whispers it to the person sitting next to them. That person whispers it to the next and so on, down the line.

Quite often the last one in the line gets a different message. It isn't the same as it was at the beginning. This game can be a lot of fun. Can you suggest why a different message often reaches the end of the line? What could you do to make sure that the message stays the same?

People who carry messages for other people are called messengers. They have to be sure that the messages they give are the right ones, and that the messages get to the right people.

Please tell Miss Jackson in class 2 that I won't be at the meeting until 2.30.

Where did you say she was, and what time did you say?

I'll write it down for you to give her.

Have you ever been a messenger? When you carry a message for someone else, it is not your message. The message is not from you, even though you are carrying it. You are the messenger.

Allah's messages

Muslims believe that Allah gave messages to many thousands of people, who lived in every country and in every period of history. Muslims call these people prophets. Prophets are people who carry messages from Allah to all people, everywhere. They are Allah's messengers.

According to Muslims, Allah has sent prophets ever since people first lived on this planet. Nobody knows the names of all these prophets. But Muslims believe that they know the names of many of the more important ones.

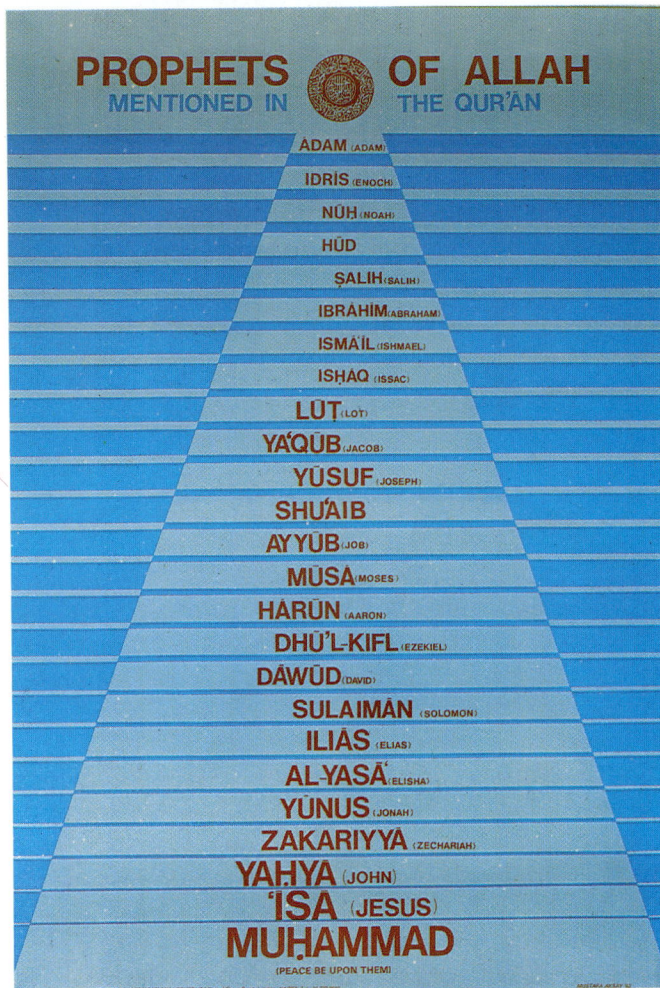

PROPHETS OF ALLAH
MENTIONED IN THE QUR'AN

ADAM (ADAM)
IDRIS (ENOCH)
NŪH (NOAH)
HŪD
ṢĀLIH (SALIH)
IBRĀHĪM (ABRAHAM)
ISMĀ'ĪL (ISHMAEL)
ISHĀQ (ISSAC)
LŪT (LOT)
YA'QUB (JACOB)
YŪSUF (JOSEPH)
SHU'AIB
AYYŪB (JOB)
MŪSA (MOSES)
HĀRŪN (AARON)
DHŪ'L-KIFL (EZEKIEL)
DĀWŪD (DAVID)
SULAIMĀN (SOLOMON)
ILIĀS (ELIAS)
AL-YASĀ' (ELISHA)
YŪNUS (JONAH)
ZAKARIYYĀ (ZECHARIAH)
YAHYA (JOHN)
'ISA (JESUS)
MUHAMMAD
(PEACE BE UPON THEM)

See if you can find any names on this chart that you have heard before. Perhaps you could talk to your teacher about what you know about any of these Muslim prophets. Did you notice that Muhammad is the last and the most important prophet?

The Qur'an

The Muslims' holy book is the Qur'an. Muslims believe that the Qur'an is the message which Allah sent to Muhammad.

Allah didn't write the message down. Muslims believe that an angel called Gabriel gave the message to Muhammad. Muhammad didn't write the message down either. However, he did remember the message, even though it was very long. Muhammad told other people exactly what the angel had told him and they wrote it down, word for word. This is how Muhammad made sure that the message would not get changed.

It took a long time for Muhammad to receive the complete message from the Angel Gabriel. He needed a very good memory to make sure that he could recite it to others.

Muslims believe that this message has never been changed. They believe that it is still exactly as Allah revealed it to Muhammad a long time ago.

Muhammad lived in Arabia when he received Allah's messages from the Angel Gabriel. That is why the Qur'an is written in the Arabic language. Today, Muslims live in many different countries and speak lots of different languages. While learning their own language, most Muslims also learn to speak or recite Arabic. They do this so that they can read the Qur'an.

When Muslims read the Qur'an in Arabic, they believe they are hearing the message of Allah just as it was given to Muhammad. For most Muslims, the message of the Qur'an is not exactly the same if it is translated into another language. Of course, most of them believe that it is better to hear the message in your own language than not at all. People who do not know Arabic could not understand this message unless it was translated into the language which they speak.

Here are two pages from the Qur'an in Arabic and English. If you can read the Arabic, perhaps you might like to read it out to your friends.

The Qur'an is arranged in chapters. Muslims call each of these chapters a surah. There are 114 chapters in the Qur'an. They are not arranged in the order in which Muhammad received them, but are generally arranged according to length. The longest ones tend to be at the beginning and the shorter ones at the end of the book.

All of the chapters, except one, begin with the Bismillah. That is the name that Muslims use for the verse at the beginning of each chapter. The Arabic word 'bismillah' means 'in the name of Allah'. Here is the whole of the Bismillah, in Arabic and English.

In the name of Allah,
Most Gracious,
Most Merciful

بِسْمِ اللّٰهِ الرَّحْمٰنِ الرَّحِيمِ

The picture below shows the first two pages of the Qur'an. Unlike English, Arabic is read from right to left across the page. Also, a book in Arabic opens where a book in English would end. This means that surah 1 of the Qur'an is on the right-hand page while surah 2 starts on the left-hand one. Both surahs start with the Bismillah. Can you pick it out?

Muslims do not use pictures to illustrate their Qur'an because they believe that Allah has told them not to make and worship idols. An idol is any object or person that is worshipped instead of Allah, and pictures could be used as idols. Muslims believe that if they make pictures or statues of anything or anybody, people may pray to these objects and not to Allah. That is why each page may be beautifully decorated with patterns and different kinds of writing, but you will not find any pictures of living things.

By not having pictures in their Qur'ans or in their mosques, Muslims are stressing two important beliefs.

- Allah created all things. People should not try to copy Allah's creation.
- Only Allah should be worshipped. People should not pray in front of any pictures or sculptures.

Many Muslims treat the Qur'an as something very special.

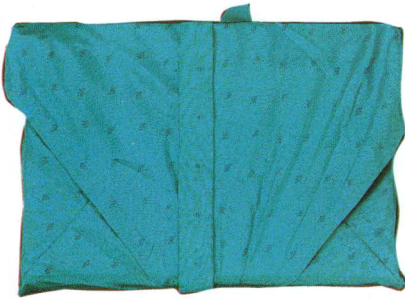

They may wrap it in a piece of clean cloth.

They may also keep it on a high shelf, to be sure that no other book is above it.

They may always wash before they touch the Qur'an.

They may place it on a stand when they read it, and make sure that it does not touch the floor.

They may try not to turn their backs on the book, when they are leaving the room where it is kept, and many may kiss the Qur'an after reading it.

Rashida gets a special gift

One day Rashida was talking with her mother. She had lots of things to talk about and lots of questions to ask.

Just then, she saw a Qur'an on a high shelf. Rashida thought for a moment and then said, 'Why can't we read the Qur'an in English? That would make it much easier.'

Mother said, 'The Qur'an isn't the Qur'an unless it is written in Arabic. The words in your book are the very words sent by Allah to the Prophet Muhammad (peace be upon him) and they have never been changed.'

'There are English Qur'ans,' said Rashida. 'I've seen them. We have one in school.'

'Yes,' said Mother. 'There are books that people have translated from Arabic into other languages but they are not the real Qur'an. The only true Qur'an is the one we all read in Arabic.'

'Well, you can get other holy books in different languages,' said Rashida.

'Yes, I know,' said Mother. 'Other holy books have been sent by Allah, but when the people alter the language they often change the meaning without realising they have done it. We will always keep the Qur'an in the language used when Allah sent it to us.'

'What about the Qur'ans I've seen in English?' asked Rashida. 'What use are they if they are not real?'

Mother replied, 'Many people do not read Arabic, so they can't read the real Qur'an. The English books you have seen are written for people who want to know about the Qur'an, but they can't read it for themselves. As long as they don't think it is the real thing, it is good for them to read it because it helps them to understand our religion.'

'The Prophet must have been a very clever man to write a book like that,' said Rashida.

'He was a very good man,' Mother said, 'but he didn't really write the Qur'an.'

'No, I know that,' said Rashida. 'Father told me how the Angel Gabriel came to Muhammad (peace be upon him) for the first time in a cave and told him to recite the message of Allah.'

'Yes, that's right,' said Mother. 'As you know, like many people in those days, the Prophet never learned to read or write. The Angel Gabriel came to Muhammad (peace be upon him) lots of times. It took 22 years altogether. The Prophet eventually repeated all the words so that they could be written down and put into a book.'

'I do think he must have been a clever man,' said Rashida.

'Well, he was very special,' said Mother. 'You know, I think the time is right for me to give you something special. I think you have proved you are grown up enough to understand and appreciate it.' She went upstairs and came down carrying a small parcel.

'This belonged to your grandfather,' she said. 'It was given to him by his father and he told me to save it and give it to you when I thought the time was right.'

'What is it?' asked Rashida.

'It is a very precious Qur'an,' replied Mother.

'But Grandfather has already given me a Qur'an,' said Rashida.

'Yes,' said Mother. 'I know. He bought that one so you could start learning to read it. This one is very old and has been in the family for many years. Your grandfather treasured it as did his father before him. He wanted you to have it because he thought you would look after it the way he did.'

Rashida washed her hands, pulled her dupatta over her head and took the book. She opened it and looked at the richly patterned pages. 'It's beautiful,' she said. 'I will keep it to read on very special occasions.'

That night when Rashida lay in bed she looked up at the shelf in her room. The two Qur'ans were side by side, the one she read every day and the one her mother had given her that afternoon. She felt very proud that her grandfather had wanted her to have his Qur'an. Perhaps one day she would be giving it to her grandchild.

Smiling to herself, Rashida fell asleep.

Obeying commands

Sometimes we have to obey other people, and do what they tell us to do. Sometimes it is very important to obey people in authority. For example, some very bad accidents can happen if people do not obey all the traffic police officer's directions for pedestrians and cars.

People can also obey rules. The policewoman in the picture is obeying some rules as she directs the traffic. If there were no rules for the police and for drivers and pedestrians nobody would know what others on the road are likely to do. Then there would be some terrible accidents.

Most people have to obey some rules every day. We have rules:
    in the games we play,
    in our families,
    in the community.

Muslims believe that they should obey Allah, and that Allah's commands are written in the Qur'an. They believe that all Allah's commands are good commands, and that obeying these commands helps them:

to know Allah a little better,
to feel close to Allah,
to avoid the punishment of Allah,
to gain favour with Allah,
to live in peace with all people,
to live better lives in this life and in the after-life.

Being a Muslim means obeying Allah.

Prayer

For Muslims, one of Allah's most important commands is to pray. When Muslims pray each day they are obeying Allah, and they believe that they should pray at least five times each day. Performing these five daily prayers is called Salah. Salah is a way of obeying Allah.

For many Muslims, offering prayer to Allah at set times each day is an important part of their life. When it is time for prayer, they may stop what they are doing and perform the prayer. They may be at home, at school, at work, in the street or at the mosque.

Because it is important to pray in a very clean place, lots of Muslims have a special mat on which to pray. They may carry this with them, so that they can use it to be sure that the area where they pray is clean.

Rules for prayer

Muslims have special rules about when to pray and how to pray. As you read about some of these rules, see if you can find several reasons which Muslims might give to explain why they pray so often.

When Muslims pray

Of course, Muslims can pray at any time and in any place. However, there are rules about the five special prayers each day. Each of the five prayers has its own Arabic name and its own special time in which it must be performed. You can find out names and times of prayers on the next page.

As you look at these names of the prayers and at the times when they take place, you may notice that they are linked to the movement of the earth around the sun. You may also know that the lengths of day and night change from day to day. In winter, daylight is short and darkness is long. In summer it is the other way around. Sunrise and sunset, therefore, come at different clock times as the seasons change so the prayer after sunset, for example, will take place much later in summer than in winter. This is why there are clocks in most mosques showing people what the correct clock time is for their prayer.

Perhaps you could find out why days are longer in summer than in winter.

Salah

NAMES OF EACH PRAYER	TIMES FOR EACH PRAYER
Fajr	from dawn until just before sunrise
Zuhr	after midday until later in the afternoon
'Asr	in the afternoon until just before sunset
Maghrib	after sunset until daylight ends
'Isha	night until midnight or dawn

How Muslims pray

For Muslims, prayer is a ritual. Rituals are special things that people do over and over again. As we know, prayer is a very important part of a Muslim's life and many Muslims perform this ritual five times a day.

Muslim prayer rituals combine special words, actions and thoughts.

Some people sit quietly on their own before the prayer ritual begins. During this time they may think about the greatness and mercy of Allah, and recite to themselves the Bismillah or other words from the Qur'an. Muslims use this time of preparation for prayer to fix their thoughts on Allah before they join in the prayer.

There are rules about how to perform the prayer. Following these rules is also an important way of obeying Allah.

Wudu

Muslims should wash before they pray. This ritual washing before prayer is called wudu. They wash their mouths, noses, faces, arms, heads and feet.

If there is no water about, then some Muslims may do a shorter form of wudu using sand, but of course they will not put the sand in their mouths or noses.

Washing like this helps Muslims to remember some of their beliefs about Allah. They believe that Allah is perfect and pure in all things, and the washing reminds them that they must try to be pure and clean in all of their life.

There are special rules for wudu. This special order for the ritual washing is set out in the chart below.

First declare your intention to prepare for prayer by reciting the Bismillah

Wash both hands up to wrists, three times.

Rinse mouth thoroughly three times.

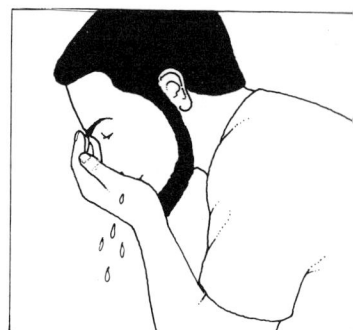

Wash tip of nose...

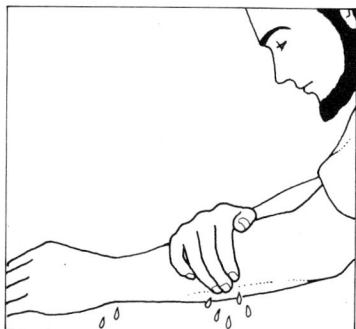

Wash right arm then left arm thoroughly from wrist to elbow three times.

Move palm of wet hand over head, starting from the top of forehead to the back...

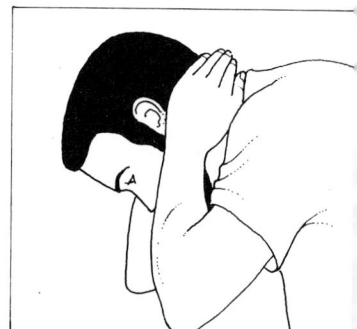

O Believers, when you rise to offer the Salah you must wash your faces and hands and arms up to the elbows and wipe your heads with wet hands and wash your feet up to the ankles.

Surah 5:6

يَٰأَيُّهَا الَّذِينَ ءَامَنُوا إِذَا قُمْتُمْ إِلَى الصَّلَوٰةِ فَاغْسِلُوا وُجُوهَكُمْ وَأَيْدِيَكُمْ إِلَى ٱلْمَرَافِقِ وَٱمْسَحُوا بِرُءُوسِكُمْ وَأَرْجُلَكُمْ

.. and nostrils, three times.

Wash face three times from right ear to left ear and from forehead to throat.

... and pass both hands over the back of the head to the neck.

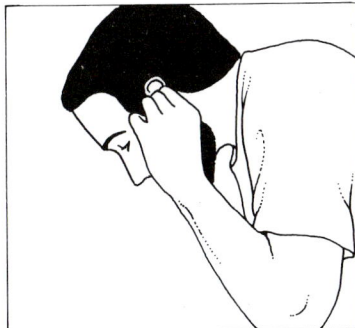

Rub wet fingers into the grooves and holes of both ears and rub the wet thumbs behind the ears.

Wash both feet thoroughly, starting with the right foot.

Rak'ah

We know that Muslims have rules about when to pray and what to do before prayer. They also have some rules about what to do and say during prayer.

Each prayer time is divided into several parts and each part is called a rak'ah. This is a series of movements and words. Muslims perform a different number of rak'ahs at each of the five times of prayer. Different Muslim groups may perform the prayer in different ways. In whatever way they pray, the idea is the same.

RULES FOR A RAK'AH

1. Stand at the edge of the prayer mat, facing towards the city of Makkah in Arabia.

   Say aloud or silently, which of the five prayers you are about to perform.

2. Men usually put their hands up to their ears. Women lift their hands up to their shoulders.

   Say the Arabic words: اَللّٰهُ اَكْبَرُ

   In English this means: *Allah is the Greatest.*

3. Men put their right hand on their left hand, just below the navel or on the chest. Women put their hands on their chests.

   Recite the Arabic words:

   سُبْحَانَكَ اللّٰهُمَّ وَبِحَمْدِكَ وَتَبَارَكَ اسْمُكَ وَتَعَالٰى جَدُّكَ وَلَا اِلٰهَ غَيرُكَ

   In English this means: *O Allah, glory and praise are for you, and blessed is your name, and exalted is your majesty; there is no god but you.*

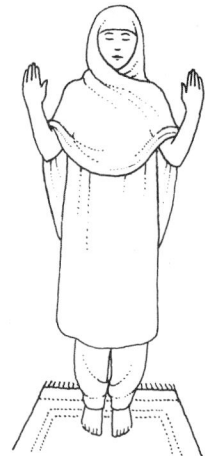

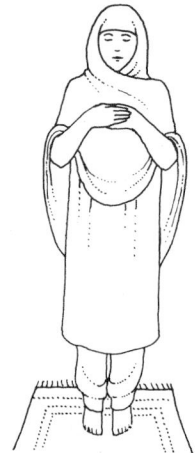

Then recite some more verses from the Qur'an.

4. Bow from the hips, so that the back is horizontal to the ground. Place hands on knees.

   Recite the Arabic words:

   a) اَللّٰهُ اَكْبَرُ   b) سُبْحَانَ رَبِيَ الْعَظِيمِ

   In English this means:
   a) *Allah is the Greatest.*
   b) *Glory to my Lord, the Great.*

   Repeat these words three times.

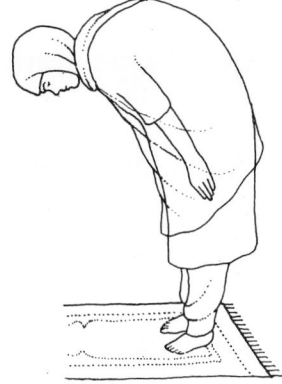

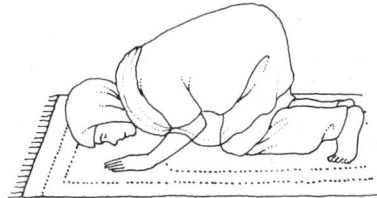

5. Stand up straight again.

   Recite the Arabic words:

   a) سَمِعَ اللّٰهُ لِمَنْ حَمِدَه   b) رَبَّنَا لَكَ الْحَمْدُ

   In English this means:
   a) *Allah hears those who praise him.*
   b) *Our Lord, praise be to you.*

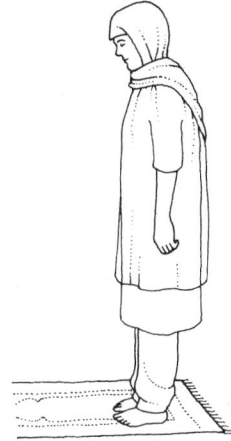

6. Go down on to the prayer mat with forehead, nose, palms of both hands and knees touching the floor.

   Recite the Arabic words:

   a) سُبْحَانَ رَبِّيَ الأَعْلٰى   b) اَللّٰهُ اَكْبَرُ

   In English this means:
   a) *Allah is the Greatest.*
   b) *Glory to my Lord, the Highest.*

   Repeat these words three times.

7. Sit upright with knees bent and palms of hands resting on knees. After a short rest, bow down to floor again, as in number 6.

Recite the Arabic words:

a) اَللّٰهُ اَكَبَرُ

b) سُبْحَانَ رَبِّيَ الْاَعْلٰى

In English this means:
a) *Allah is the Greatest.*   b) *Glory to my Lord, the Highest.*

Repeat the second line of these words three times.

8. When the prayer is finished and while sitting on the floor, turn the head to face the right.

Recite the Arabic words:

اَلسَّلَامُ عَلَيْكُم وَرَحْمَةُ اللّٰهِ

In English this means:
Peace and the mercy of Allah be on you.

Turn the head to face the left and repeat the same words.

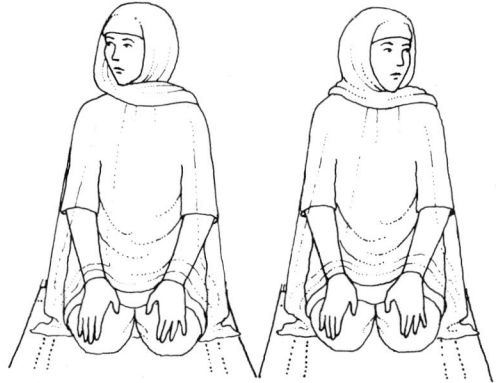

This completes one rak'ah. What happens next depends on how many rak'ahs are included in the prayer. Different words and actions will take place at this point, depending on whether the prayer has two, three or four rak'ahs.

It is very important for Muslims to follow the rules for prayer correctly. This is because they believe that praying at set times and in these special ways is a way of obeying the commands of Allah. They believe that they have been told to perform the prayer in the same way as the Prophet Muhammad.

2 Muslim Family Life

Marriage

Most people want to live with someone else. We do not like feeling lonely. Most of us live with our families.

Loving and being loved by other people is a very important part of our lives and most people begin learning about this in their families.

Most new families begin when two people get married. Getting married is usually a very happy and exciting time when two people agree to live together and start a new family.

Most communities of people in the world have special rules, ceremonies and customs which guide and help people when they agree to marry each other. Some of the rules may be part of the law of the country. The laws may say who can conduct marriage ceremonies and at what times and places they can happen. People living in the same country have to obey the laws of that country, but they may have very different ceremonies and customs for when they get married.

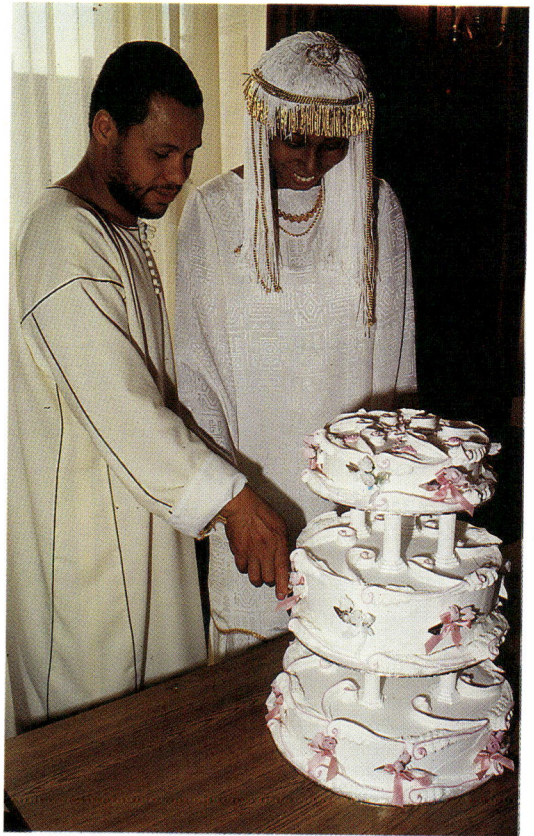

Some of the ceremonies and customs are part of the preparation for marriage. They help couples to get ready for their marriage. For example:

- announcing to families and the community that the couple intends to get married,
- having parties,
- giving presents,
- visiting relatives and friends.

Other ceremonies and customs are part of the day of the marriage. They mark the beginning of a new family, as the couple get married. For example:

- joining in a special religious ceremony,
- signing contracts and other documents,
- having a wedding feast,
- dressing up in wedding clothes,
- throwing confetti, flowers, rice and other things over the couple being married.

Muslim marriages

Most Muslims believe that marriage and living together in families is very important. They believe that it is the will of Allah that men and women should live together and care for children within a family.

Muslims have a very old story about Allah making the very first man and woman to live on this planet. They share this story with some other religious people – especially Jews and Christians. Perhaps you have heard a story very much like this one; some people call it the story of Adam and Eve. Muslims call it the story of Adam and Hawa. This story suggests to Muslims that Allah intends people to live together in families. They also believe that the story shows that marriages are more likely to succeed if the couple share their obedience to Allah.

The Story of Adam and Hawa

Allah created the heaven and the earth and everything in them was ready. The sun was shining, the clouds were floating by, the fishes were swimming, the birds were flying. Animals hopped and jumped, and plants blossomed and fruits grew ripe. The angels were ready because Allah had told them what He was about to do.

Allah said to the angels, 'I will place a representative on earth.'

The angels said, 'Will you put someone there who will only cause trouble and shed blood; while we praise You and obey You?'

But Allah said, 'I know what you do not know.'

Allah began to create a human being. From the wet water He took a bit and from the dry earth a bit. Then He created a man from a mixture of these. Then He, be He exalted and glorified, breathed from His spirit into the man and the man came to life. Allah gave this man the name Adam.

Allah taught Adam all the names of things. Allah helped Adam to understand how to use them. Adam looked at the sky and saw a great light, the sun. When the darkness came he saw smaller lights – the moon, the stars, and the planets. He had the knowledge of day and night, and he knew the difference between them.

All around Adam was a garden – full of shade, flowers and fruits of all kinds. With the gift of his body and its senses and limbs Adam went through the garden touching, tasting, seeing, hearing and remembering all that Allah had taught him. Allah showed him all the plants and animals. Allah told him which to use and how, and which not to use. Adam heard the sounds of the earth and smelled the smells and each thing was a reminder to him of Allah.

All around Adam was a creation of beautiful things. But Adam had no companion. He could not share the creation with any other person. So Allah created a woman, and the woman's name was Hawa. She was a wife and companion for him.

Allah said to them, 'Oh Adam! You and your wife may live in the garden. Eat from where you wish but do not draw near this tree or you will be among the unjust!'

But Shaytan, a disobedient spirit, was waiting for them. He whispered to them, saying, 'Your Lord only told you not to touch this tree because He did not want you to become angels or live forever.' When Adam and Hawa heard Shaytan they believed what he told them. Now the garden and all its gifts seemed small and they wanted more, and with that Shaytan deceived them, and they forgot Allah's warning.

They took one of the fruits from the tree, but as soon as they had tasted the fruit they were ashamed of what they had done. Adam and Hawa did not want Allah to see their mistake so they took leaves and tried to cover themselves to hide from Allah.

Even when they forgot Allah, Allah did not forget them. He said to Adam, 'Did I not forbid you that tree and tell you that Shaytan is truly your enemy?' They said, 'Our Lord, we have wronged ourselves and if You do not forgive and have mercy upon us, we will be completely lost.'

Allah ordered both of them to get out of the garden. They had lost the peace Allah had given them. Now the earth would be their home for a while. They would have to work hard in their lifetime there. And finally they would die. Allah promised them that if they followed his guidance, they would not lose their way and be miserable. In the end, they would be returned once again to Allah. The earth was only meant to be their home for a short time.

Adam and Hawa left the garden and began their more difficult life on the earth. They did not forget what Allah had said and how Shaytan had tricked them. They always had a bad feeling in their heart concerning Shaytan.

Together Adam and Hawa had children, and cared for them and told them about Allah's promises to them. They warned their children about Shaytan. They taught their children to be Allah's representatives on the earth, and to care for the earth on which they lived. Some of the children listened and some did not.

The children of Adam and Hawa grew up and had their own children, and their children had more children, and in this way the world was filled with people.

Everyone was created from one man, Adam, and one woman, Hawa. From these two came all the nations and all the tribes on earth. The ones who follow Shaytan are miserable and unhappy and enter the fire. But the ones who follow Allah and His messengers come back to the garden. And that is Allah's promise. We come from Allah and He is our beginning and we return to Allah and He is our end.

Muslim marriage rules

Muslims believe that they must obey the laws of the country in which they live and the laws of Allah about marriage. Here are some of the laws about marriage which many Muslims try to keep. In some Muslim countries, like Pakistan, these rules may be part of the law of the country. In other countries, Muslims may choose to keep them because of their religious belief.

SOME RULES FOR MUSLIM WOMEN

1. Muslim women have the main responsibility for looking after and caring for their family.
2. Muslim women may not marry men who are not Muslims.
3. Muslim women should not have more than one husband at a time.

SOME RULES FOR MUSLIM MEN

1. Muslim men should pay some money to the women they marry. This is usually called a dowry.
2. Muslim men may marry women who are not Muslims, if they are practising Christians or Jews.
3. A Muslim man should not force his non-Muslim wife to become a Muslim.
4. In special cases, and if the law of the country allows it, a Muslim man may have up to four wives at a time, as long as he treats them all the same.

Muslim men and women are taught that it is wrong to live with and start a family with someone to whom they are not married.

Marriage customs

Because Muslims live in lots of different countries, they also enjoy a variety of ceremonies and customs when they get married. Lots of these are shared by other people in the communities where they live. Muslims living in India, Britain, Pakistan, Arabia, Egypt or Malaysia may have very different marriage customs. Many of these customs are just a lot of fun. They are not part of the rules of Islam for marriage.

Some families have special preparations a few days before the marriage takes place. These preparations may include:

- painting patterns on the bride's hands and feet with red dye,
- receiving gifts from relatives and friends,
- preparing extra food for the wedding feast,
- joining with friends to sing Islamic songs.

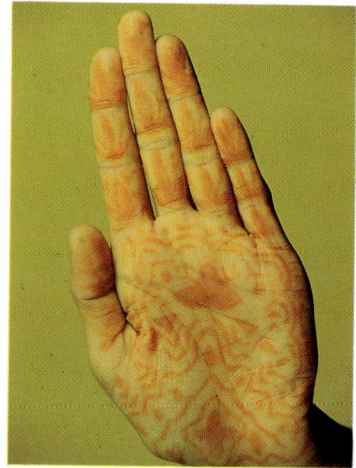

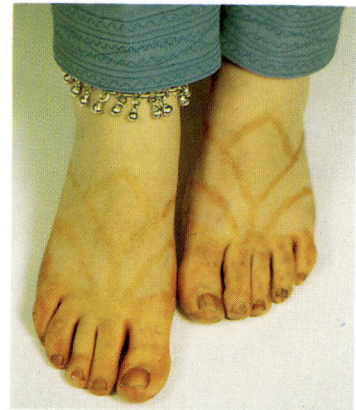

Some Muslim families from Pakistan, for example, tease the bridegroom when he arrives at the marriage reception. He often finds that the bride's sisters are sitting in his place. He has to persuade them to move. They laugh at him and refuse to move until he gives them a gift of money.

The marriage ceremony

A Muslim marriage ceremony may be held in the home or at a mosque.

For many Muslims a marriage is not just two people starting a new family. It is joining together two existing families. The families of the bride and the groom feel that they are linked together by the marriage of their children.

Many marriage customs express this idea of linking families together. In many countries the parents help in choosing the partners for the marriage. They believe that young people need a lot of help when they choose their marriage partners. They also believe that it is important for all the members of each family to feel that they are a part of the new family.

On the day of the marriage the groom may lead his family to the bride's house. Of course, they will all be dressed in their very best clothes. The men go into one room and the women into another.

Any adult Muslim man, who knows what to do, may conduct the wedding. However, it is usually the imam, who leads the prayer at the mosque, who does this. The imam goes to the girl first and asks her if she is willing to marry the boy. Sometimes the imam asks her this three times to make sure that she does want to marry the boy. The

imam then goes to the boy and asks him to recite some words from the Qur'an. The boy is then asked if he is willing to marry the girl. When they all agree, the imam declares that they are married. They all sign the marriage contract and the bride and groom are given a marriage certificate.

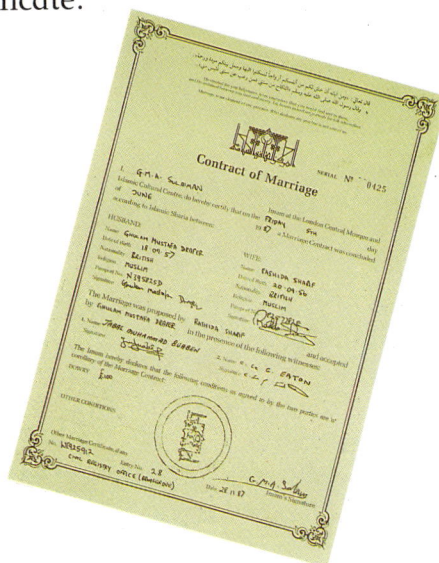

Food and drink

Most of us eat a lot of our food at home, and eating and drinking together is an important time of the day for many families. Sharing in the buying, cooking, serving and eating of food can also be a very enjoyable part of living together as a family.

There are lots of different things to eat and drink, and there are lots of different ways of cooking, serving and eating food. All the members of a family may not like eating and drinking the same things. We all have our likes and dislikes about food.

Sometimes people from one country don't like eating the kinds of food that people from another country enjoy. Some people like eating lots of different kinds of foods. They enjoy food and drink that is different from the food and drink they have at home.

Many people have some rules about what they should and should not eat and drink. Perhaps your family has some rules like this. If you do have rules about what to eat and what not to eat, perhaps you could talk with your friends and teachers about them.

Muslim rules about food and drink

> *Then, you should eat the flesh of the animal over which Allah's name has been mentioned, if you sincerely believe in His Revelations.*
>
> *Surah 16:114*

فَكُلُوا مِمَّا ذُكِرَ اسْمُ اللَّهِ عَلَيْهِ إِن كُنتُم بِآيَتِهِ مُؤْمِنِين

Muslims believe that Allah created the world as a home for all people. They also believe that Allah intends people to enjoy the good food and drink available on this planet. Allah also guides people away from eating and drinking things which are unhealthy.

Many Muslim scientists, doctors and others study very hard to discover which foods and drinks are good for people and which are harmful. Some work very hard to help people who become sick from eating or drinking things which are harmful.

Many Muslims also believe that they are obeying Allah when they try to bring good food and drink to those who do not have enough to eat or drink.

ISLAMIC RELIEF AGENCY
الوكالة الاسلامية للاغاثة

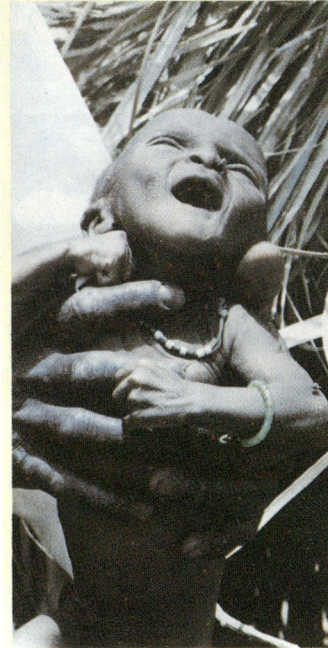

Many Muslim families also have rules about which foods are allowed and which are forbidden by Allah. Things that are allowed are called halal. Things that are forbidden are called haram. Most fish and fresh vegetables are halal. However, there are some special rules about what kinds of meat are either halal or haram.

Here are some of the kinds of animals which Muslims believe are haram. They should not be eaten as meat.

- pigs,
- animals that eat other animals for food,
- animals and birds that died naturally or from diseases,
- animals strangled to death,
- animals not killed for food in the proper Muslim way,
- animals killed for food without someone reciting the name of Allah,
- animals' blood.

In lots of towns and cities you may see some halal butcher shops. The sign outside tells Muslims that the meat they sell has been prepared according to Muslim rules, and most Muslim families try to buy all their meat from these halal shops.

O Believers, wine, gambling, (ungodly) shrines and divining devices are all abominable works of Shaytan: therefore refrain from these so that you may attain true success. Indeed Shaytan intends to sow enmity and hatred among you by means of wine and gambling, and to prevent you from the remembrance of Allah and from Salah. Will you not, therefore, abstain from these things?

Surah 5:90,91

يَا أَيُّهَا الَّذِينَ اٰمَنُوا اِنَّمَا الْخَمْرُ وَالْمَيْسِرُ
وَالْاَنْصَابُ وَالْاَزْلَامُ
رِجْسٌ مِّنْ عَمَلِ الشَّيْطٰنِ
فَاجْتَنِبُوهُ لَعَلَّكُمْ تُفْلِحُونَ
اِنَّمَا يُرِيدُ الشَّيْطٰنُ
اَنْ يُوقِعَ بَيْنَكُمُ الْعَدَاوَةَ وَالْبَغْضَاءَ فِي
الْخَمْرِ وَالْمَيْسِرِ وَيَصُدَّكُمْ عَنْ ذِكْرِ اللّٰهِ
وَعَنِ الصَّلٰوةِ فَهَلْ اَنْتُمْ مُّنْتَهُونَ

Most Muslims never drink wine or other alcoholic drinks. They believe that alcohol and harmful drugs are forbidden because they are unhealthy. They also know that the misuse of these drugs causes a lot of trouble for individuals and for communities. The drinking of alcohol and the misuse of drugs are therefore haram.

3 Muslim Personal Life

Our own life

We all have to live our own life. Living our own life often means making choices. Sometimes we can choose what we wear, what we eat, what we say, and what we do.

Sometimes we may not have any choice. Many things can take people's choice away from them. For example, people who are poor, ill or handicapped, or who live in a country at war, may have little choice about what they wear, eat, say or do.

Sometimes other people tell us what to do, say, eat or wear. Sometimes we enjoy doing what other people tell us, but we may also not enjoy being told. We like to make our own choices.

Sometimes making a choice is very hard. We are not sure what we want to do, or we are not sure what other people think about our choices.

Sometimes we have to choose between right and wrong. This may not be easy. We may not know what is right or wrong. But even when we believe we know what is right, we may not want to do it. Making choices is part of living your own personal life.

Muslims

Muslims believe that all people should live as Allah wants them to live. They believe that Muhammad lived that way. He chose to worship and obey Allah. Muhammad is the most important Muslim who has ever lived. For Muslims, he is the best example of a good person, because he chose to live as Allah said people should.

Reading and studying the story of Muhammad helps Muslims to make good choices in their personal life. Most Muslims believe that if they know the Qur'an and follow the example of Muhammad, they will know how to live their own lives. They will know what to wear, what to eat, what to say and what to do. They will know the difference between right and wrong, and they will know how to worship and obey Allah.

Muslims believe that Muhammad is the prophet who helps them to know what Allah wants them to do. For them, the Qur'an is the book where they can read Allah's messages to the Prophet about how people should live.

The story of Muhammad

The story of Muhammad is a very long story. He was born in Makkah in Arabia about the year 571 C.E., and he was about 60 years old when he died in the city of Medina. Many Muslims try to visit these two places at least once in their life. Visiting the places where he was born and where he died helps them to remember him. It may also help them to try harder to live as Muslims.

Growing up in Makkah

For most of his life Muhammad was an orphan. His father died before he was born and his mother died when he was six. Muhammad lived for a while with his grandfather and then with his uncle, Abu Talib.

When Muhammad was growing up in Makkah, it was a very busy trading city. People came from miles around to buy and sell things.

Many wealthy merchants lived in the city and so did lots of very poor and needy people. The wealthy merchants were only interested in getting richer and richer. They did very little to help the poor.

At that time most of the Arabs worshipped idols. These idols, or statues of gods, were kept in special shrines. One of the most important places for shrines was in Makkah. There, the shrines were kept inside and around the outside of a cube-shaped building, called the Ka'ba.

The honest merchant

When Muhammad was old enough, he too became a merchant. He travelled long distances with his uncle to buy and sell goods, and he soon became a very successful merchant. Many people said that his success came because he was honest and trustworthy.

One day, a widow called Khadija asked Muhammad to take charge of all her business affairs. She had heard how honest and trustworthy he was. Later Khadija and Muhammad were married. They had a family of six children.

Although Muhammad was a successful trader with a happy family, he was very sad. He was sad because so many people were dishonest and could not be trusted. He was sad because so many people were selfish and greedy, and because so many of the rich people didn't care about the very poor people. He was also sad because so many people worshipped idols. Muhammad often spent long hours in prayer and fasting, thinking about these sad things. Was there anything, he wondered, that would show people how to choose a good, rather than a bad, way of living?

Allah's messages

Muhammad often went out into the hills around Makkah to fast and pray. Sometimes he stayed in the hills for several days. One evening he was praying in a cave on Mount Hira, when suddenly, something strange appeared to him. He was frightened at first, then he realised that it was an angel. It was the Angel Gabriel.

The angel showed Muhammad some words and told him to read them. Muhammad couldn't read, but he could remember things. So he learned the words. Each time the angel visited him, Muhammad learned all the words that were recited to him.

He soon believed that the angel was giving him messages from Allah. He believed that these messages would give the answer to his questions about the ways people were living. He must remember these messages and take them to the people of Makkah.

Muslims call this first meeting between Muhammad and the Angel Gabriel, 'the Night of Power'.

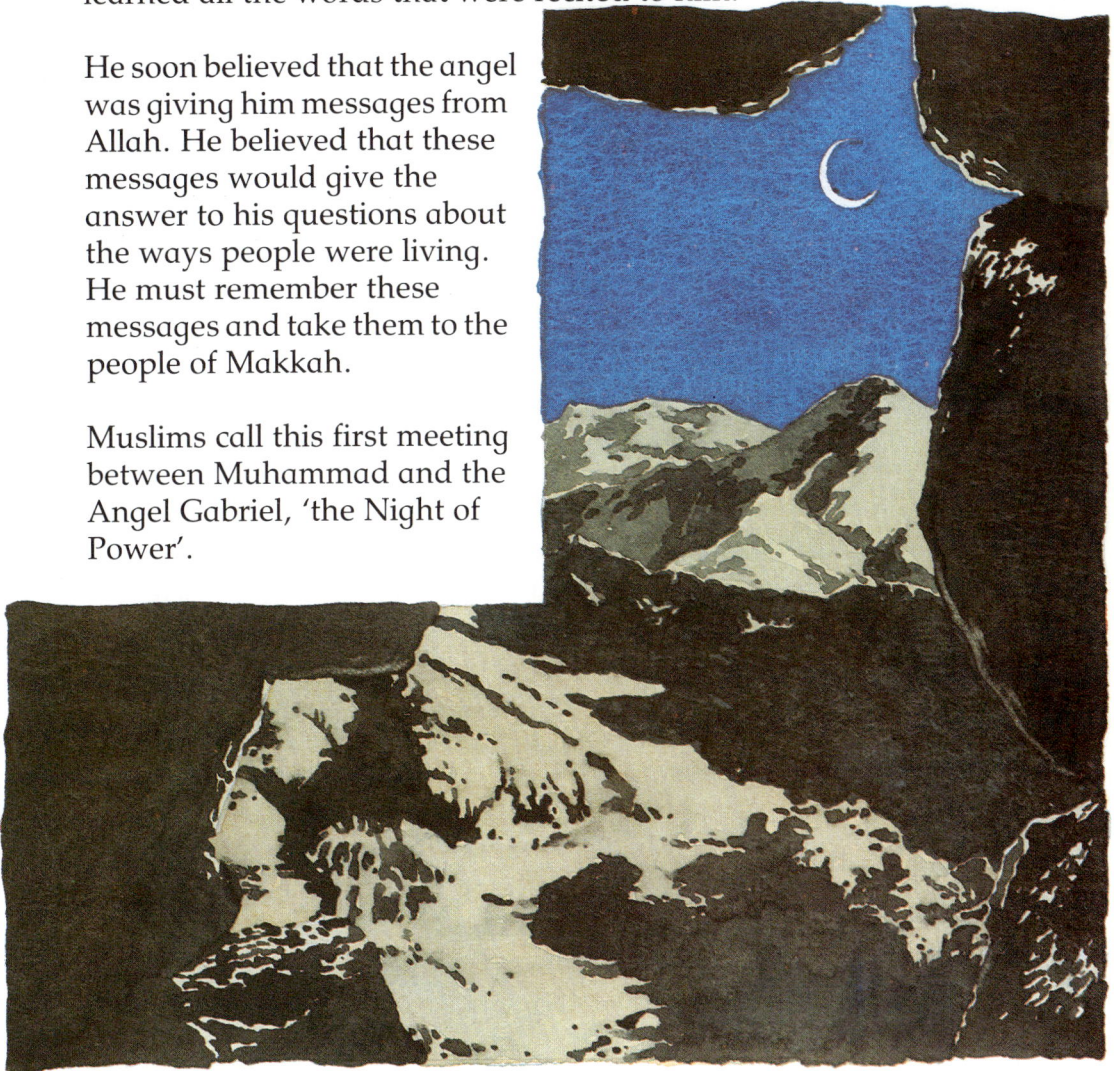

The Prophet's preaching

Muhammad believed that he was Allah's prophet, and he spent more and more time praying and preaching. For over 20 years he received messages from Allah. He memorised all these messages and preached to the people about them.

He tried to persuade people to be honest, truthful and caring. He said that helping people like orphans, widows, the poor, the old, the sick and the hungry was more valuable than money and luxury. He preached that worshipping idols was wrong and only Allah should be worshipped. He encouraged people to look for signs of Allah in the beauty of nature, in fresh running water, in growing crops and in newborn babies. Allah was to be seen in all things, he told the people.

Muhammad's preaching was also about life after death. People would be rewarded or punished for what they did in this life, he told his hearers. As people listened to Muhammad, some felt ashamed and some felt guilty. Some were angry with him. They felt that he was attacking them for the way they had chosen to live their lives.

From Makkah to Medina

Life became very difficult for Muhammad in Makkah, because he now had many enemies. He and his friends were often threatened with death, and many were locked up, beaten or left to starve.

After the death of his wife, Khadija, and his uncle, Muhammad decided to move from Makkah. Some people from the town of Yathrib heard about Muhammad and his messages from Allah. They believed that he could help them live better lives, so they invited Muhammad and his supporters to move to their town. After several years of careful planning, Muhammad and his supporters escaped from their enemies in Makkah and moved to Yathrib. Many people in Yathrib believed that Muhammad was Allah's prophet. They wanted him to teach them how to obey the will of Allah and to live in peace.

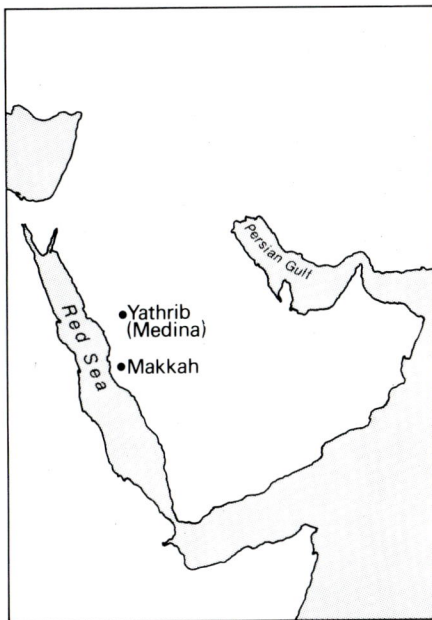

Now, Muhammad was able to put into practice everything that Allah was telling him about how people should live. Later the name of the city of Yathrib was changed. Its new name became Medinat ul-Nabi. In English this means 'the city of the Prophet', and is usually referred to as Medina.

The return to Makkah

More and more people accepted the way of Allah as Muhammad preached it to them in Medina. It seemed that only the people of Makkah were hostile to Muhammad and his teaching. One day Muhammad was convinced that Allah had commanded him to visit Makkah again. He knew that it was very dangerous, but he believed that he must obey Allah.

Muhammad and a thousand supporters set off for Makkah. They did not go as soldiers. They went as pilgrims and in peace. Many of the people in Makkah knew that Muhammad and his supporters had come in peace and a peace treaty was agreed. Muhammad and his friends were allowed to visit the Ka'ba. They were also given permission to visit the city once every year.

At one time, the rulers of Makkah broke their word. They stopped Muhammad and his friends from visiting the city. This time Muhammad went to Makkah with an army of 10,000 soldiers. They captured Makkah and at last it became a Muslim city. The Ka'ba became a place for the worship of Allah and all the idols were removed.

Today Muslims all around the world turn in the direction of the Ka'ba when they pray to Allah.

You may have noticed that the story of Muhammad does not contain any pictures of him. Do you know why this is?

Muslims do not draw, paint, or carve images of Muhammad. This is one way of showing that he must never be worshipped. Praying to or worshipping an image or a picture is called idolatry, and one of Allah's messages in the Qur'an is that idolatry is wrong. Muslims are to worship Allah and only Allah.

The story of Bilal

Although Muslims do not worship or pray to Muhammad, they do think he is the most important example of how to obey Allah. But they also read the stories of the lives of other good people. Reading these stories helps them to live their own personal lives as Allah wants. The story of Bilal, a black slave who was one of Muhammad's closest friends, is one of these stories which many Muslims read.

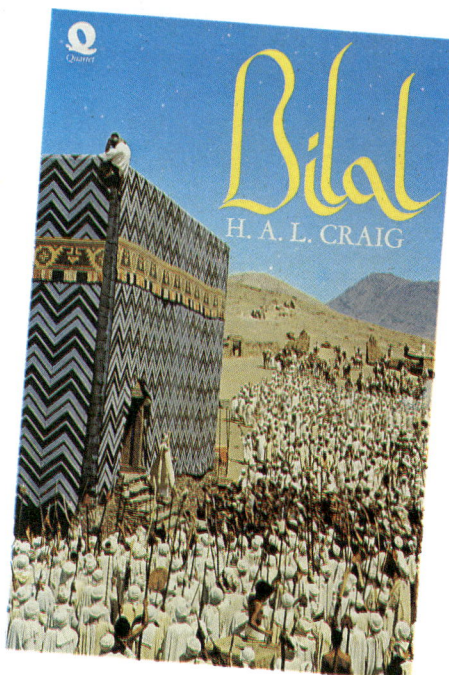

Bilal the slave

Bilal was a slave. He had to obey his master in all things, so he had no choice about how he would live his own personal life. His parents were black Africans, but they had been brought to Arabia as slaves. He too could only be a slave. When he was old enough he was sold to a new master in the market place.

Bilal, the black slave, was owned by Umaya, a wealthy merchant of Makkah, during the time when Muhammad began his preaching about Allah. As Bilal crouched in the shadows of the market place, waiting for the orders of Umaya, he heard the preaching of Muhammad and his companions.

'There is only one God,' he heard them say. 'There is no god but Allah. Allah alone is God and Allah alone is to be obeyed and worshipped.'

No wonder his master, who made money from the sale of idols, was angry.

'All people are equal,' he heard Muhammad say. 'All people are as equal as the teeth in a comb. All people, all colours, all races are equal in the sight of Allah.'

No wonder his master was angry with these preachers. 'Slaves cannot be equal with masters!' he thought.

Bilal disobeys his master

One day Bilal watched as his master, Umaya, argued with one of Muhammad's companions. 'Is Bilal, my black slave, equal with me?' asked Umaya.

'That is what Muhammad teaches as the will of Allah,' came the reply.

'Bilal! Come here!' demanded Umaya. 'Bilal, show this man the difference between a Lord of Makkah and a black slave. I order you to strike his face to teach his mouth a lesson.'

A whip was placed in Bilal's hand and he was ordered to strike the Muslim preacher. Bilal dropped the whip. People were shocked. The slave had disobeyed his master!

Bilal was tied up with ropes and left in prison over night. As he waited for his death, he thought more about the messages Muhammad was bringing from Allah. He became convinced that they were true and a deep peace came to him.

He waited for daylight and his fate at the hands of his cruel master.

Bilal is sold again

Next morning, Bilal was taken out into the heat of the desert sun. He was staked to the scorching ground and savagely whipped. People who went near him heard him repeating two words: 'One God, One God, One God.'

Later when his tormentors thought that he was almost dead they placed heavy stones on his body. Bilal felt himself being crushed to death by the large stones. Then, suddenly, he could hear voices. People were arguing. They were arguing about him. They were haggling over the price to be paid for the black slave. Somebody wanted to buy him!

The great stones were removed. Umaya was trying to revive him. Umaya now wanted him alive, because he had a buyer for this slave. Bilal, who was almost dead, was again worth money. Someone had bought him.

Bilal – a Muslim

Abu Bakr, one of Muhammad's closest companions, had bought the dying black slave. Abu Bakr and Saeed, the adopted son of Muhammad, had rescued Bilal. They took him home to care for him. Muhammad watched over the slave for days and prayed to Allah.

Many people heard of the way in which the Prophet cried as he watched the suffering slave. Gradually Bilal recovered and became stronger.

Some time later, Bilal went to see the Prophet, who invited Bilal to sit beside him. Bilal was no longer a slave. He was free. He did not have to stand. He could sit beside the Prophet as a friend and companion.

Bilal became such a close companion to Muhammad that he remained with him for the rest of the Prophet's life. He even had the privilege of calling the Prophet to prayer early each morning. He was one of Muhammad's closest and dearest friends.

When Muhammad moved to the city of Medina, Bilal went with him. There, in the city of the Prophet, Muhammad and his companions built the first mosque.

When this place of prayer was finished many of the Muslims wondered what they could use to call people to prayer. Many suggestions were made. Perhaps they could use a flag, or a bell, or a drum, or a horn, or a trumpet.

The Prophet was silent as each suggestion was made and discussed. Then Abdullah bin Zaid came to Muhammad. He had had a dream. In his dream Allah had told him to use a human voice to call the Muslims to prayer. Muhammad agreed.

'Bilal! Yours is the voice we will use.'

Unsure at first, Bilal agreed to call the people to prayer using his own loud voice.

Bilal – the muezzin

Some years later, Muhammad and the Muslims returned to Makkah where they cleared all the idols away from the Ka'ba. When this was done, Bilal climbed to the top of the Ka'ba. This was a difficult and dangerous thing to do. When he got to the top, he stood up and in a loud voice called the people to prayer.

Allah is the greatest (*2 times*)
I bear witness that there is no god
    but Allah (*2 times*)
I bear witness that Muhammad is
    Allah's messenger (*2 times*)
Come to prayer (*2 times*)
Come to salvation (*2 times*)
Allah is the greatest (*2 times*)
There is no god but Allah (*once*)

Bilal, the black slave, had become the first muezzin. A muezzin is the person who calls Muslims to prayer.

Today, in almost every mosque throughout the world, muezzins call Muslims to prayer. They are following the tradition of Bilal, the black slave, whom Muhammad once called 'a man of Paradise'. Perhaps you could talk to your friends about why Muhammad called Bilal 'a man of Paradise'.

What Muslims believe and do

We all have to live our own lives. Many people try to live out their own personal lives in accordance with certain religious beliefs and practices. Muslims try to live their lives according to the religion of Islam.

Islam is an Arabic word which, in English, means 'submission' and 'obedience'. Muslims are, therefore, people who try to submit to and obey the will of Allah. They believe Allah's will is set out in the Qur'an and that the Prophet Muhammad showed them how to obey Allah.

Of course, all Muslims do not believe exactly the same things and they do not all practise their religion in exactly the same way. A lot depends on the country where they live. Muslims living in Pakistan, Israel, Africa or Britain may live in very different ways. Also, Muslims of different ages may believe and do things in different ways. The beliefs of children, teenagers and adults are often quite different.

Certain other things may also affect the way in which particular Muslims live out their personal lives. For example:

- the family they belong to,
- the country they live in or grew up in,
- how much money they have,
- how fit and strong they are.

However, while individual Muslims have to live out their religion in their own ways, there are some important beliefs and practices which unite all Muslims in the religion of Islam.

Islamic beliefs

Many Muslims suggest that there are six beliefs which all Muslims should hold. These are often divided into three groups. Each group has its own Arabic name, which tells us what the beliefs are about.

Tauhid – Beliefs about Allah

ALLAH

Islam teaches that there is only one God. Allah is the God. Nothing else is as great as Allah. Nothing else is to be worshipped. Allah is the one and only creator who cares for and rules the whole universe.

Islam teaches that Allah knows everything about the past, the present and the future. Allah is in control of all things. Allah decides what is good and what is bad. Allah decides and knows the final destiny of all people.

Risalah – Beliefs about Allah's messengers (prophethood)

ANGELS OF ALLAH

Angels were created by Allah. They do what Allah commands. They cannot disobey Allah. Angels are seldom seen. They can appear as human beings if the will of Allah requires it.

MESSENGERS OF ALLAH

Allah has sent messengers (prophets) to remind people that there is no god but Allah. All of these prophets taught the will of Allah. They were all humans. Muhammad was Allah's last and most important prophet.

BOOKS OF ALLAH

Allah sent books of guidance through some of the prophets. The most important are the Torah (Moses), Psalms (David), Gospels (Jesus), and the Qur'an (Muhammad). Only the Qur'an exists in its pure, original form.

Akhirah – Beliefs about the next life

LIFE AFTER DEATH
Life on this planet is temporary. Death ends our human body but not our soul. At death every soul is taken by an angel to Allah. Life on earth is a preparation for the never-ending life of the soul. It is this life after death which gives meaning to life on earth.

DAY OF JUDGEMENT
Good actions are rewarded and bad actions are punished in a next life. On the Day of Judgement all souls will have to give an account to Allah for their behaviour on earth. The good will live in heaven in peace and happiness. Wrong-doers will be severely punished in hell.

The five pillars of Islam

The religion of Islam sets out five things that Muslims ought to do if they want to express the beliefs of their religion in their personal lives. These are often called the five pillars of Islam.

Perhaps you know that the word 'pillar' is another name for the posts that hold up large buildings. By calling these duties of Islam 'pillars' Muslims mean that the whole of their life stands on, or is supported by, them. Carrying out these five duties holds Muslims to their faith and helps them to live every part of their lives in obedience to the will of Allah.

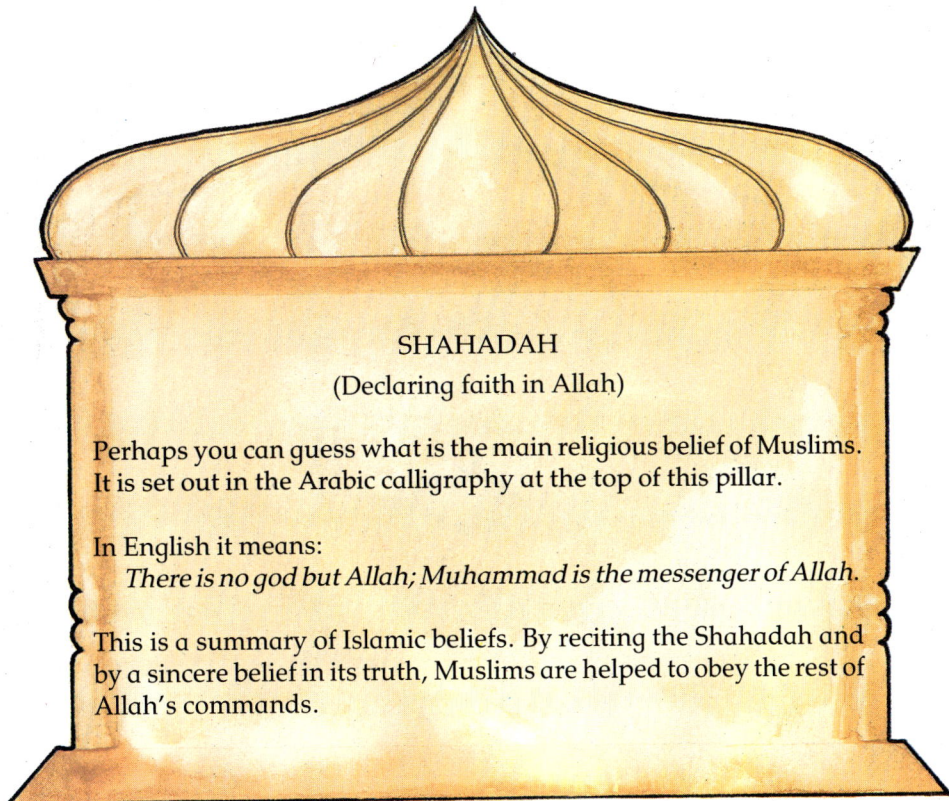

SHAHADAH
(Declaring faith in Allah)

Perhaps you can guess what is the main religious belief of Muslims. It is set out in the Arabic calligraphy at the top of this pillar.

In English it means:
There is no god but Allah; Muhammad is the messenger of Allah.

This is a summary of Islamic beliefs. By reciting the Shahadah and by a sincere belief in its truth, Muslims are helped to obey the rest of Allah's commands.

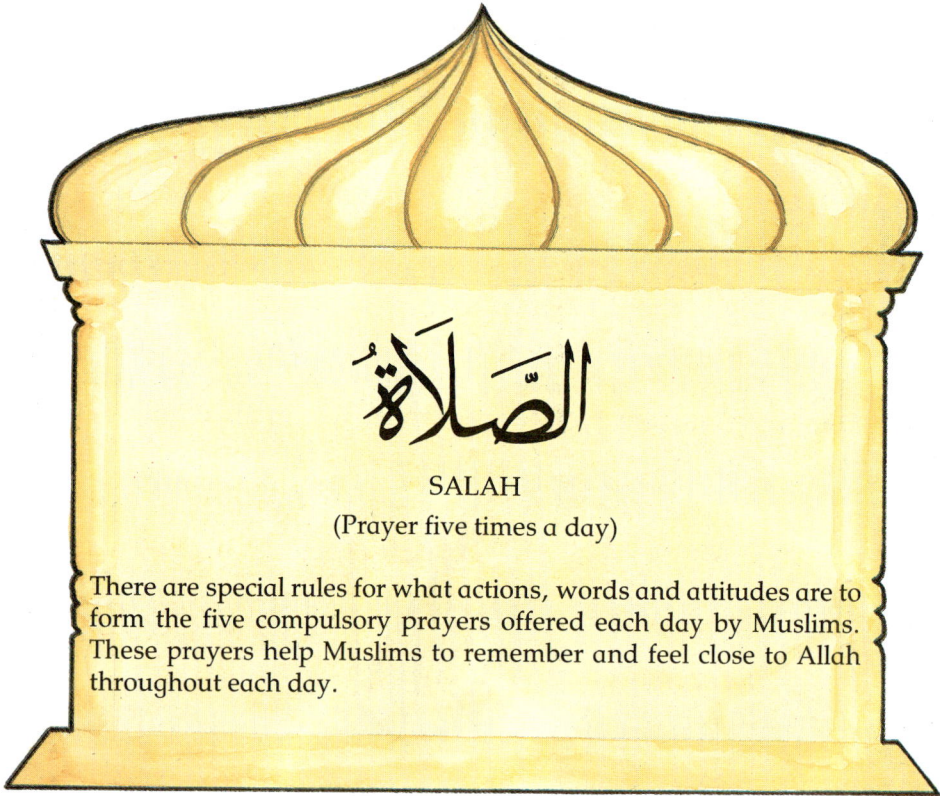

الصَّلَاةُ

SALAH

(Prayer five times a day)

There are special rules for what actions, words and attitudes are to form the five compulsory prayers offered each day by Muslims. These prayers help Muslims to remember and feel close to Allah throughout each day.

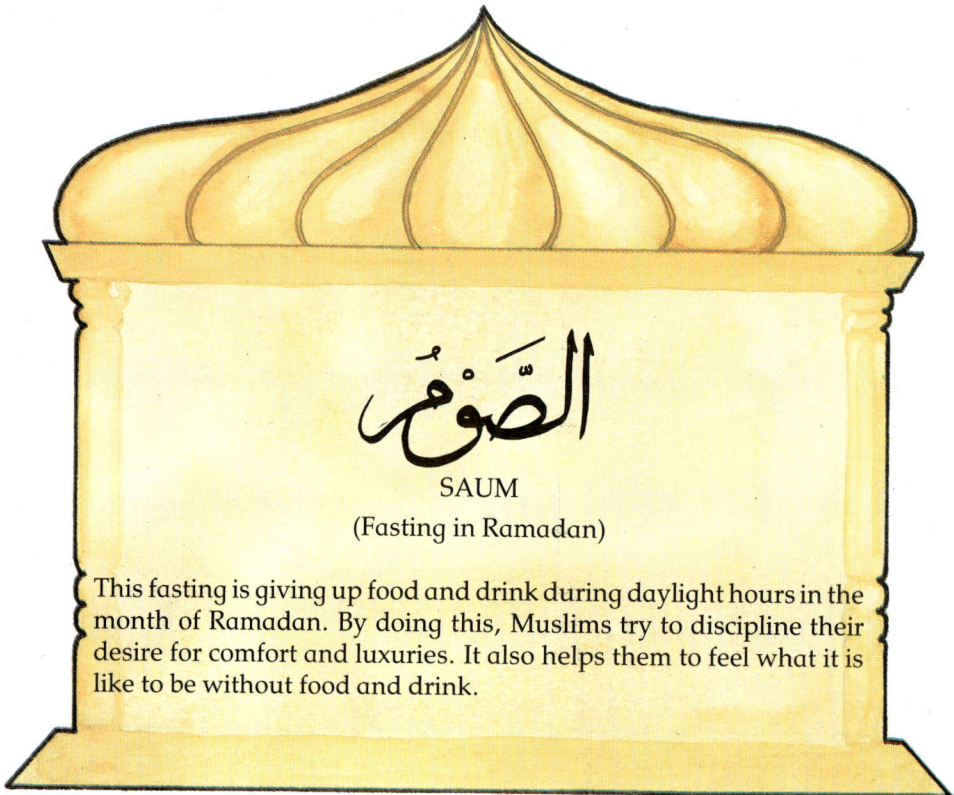

الصَّوْمُ

SAUM

(Fasting in Ramadan)

This fasting is giving up food and drink during daylight hours in the month of Ramadan. By doing this, Muslims try to discipline their desire for comfort and luxuries. It also helps them to feel what it is like to be without food and drink.

الزَّكَاة

ZAKAT

(Contributions to the welfare of others)

The word Zakat means to purify or cleanse. It refers to the giving up of a share of each person's wealth each year. The money is used to support the Muslim community and to help people in need. Making this sacrifice helps Muslims to try to be free ('cleansed') of greed and selfishness. It also helps people who are in need.

الْحَج

HAJJ

(Pilgrimage to Makkah)

Most Muslims try to go on this pilgrimage to the Ka'ba in Makkah once in their life. It takes place between the 8th and 13th of the twelfth month of the Islamic calendar. It is a time when Muslims from all around the world meet together. They all dress alike and perform several rituals. This helps them to feel members of the larger Islamic community throughout the world.

...for teachers

The material in this book is intended to help children learn about Muslims. Islamic practices and beliefs are described clearly and without any assumptions being made about any teacher's or pupil's acceptance of the Islamic religion now or in the future.

Clearly one book cannot deal with every aspect of Islam. This book, along with others in the set, points to important features of Islam and gives pupils some clear guidelines for continuing their exploration of this religion within the context of R.E. in schools.

This book is the second in a set of four books. It is intended for use with pupils aged 9–11 years, and is therefore best suited for use in upper primary R.E. courses.

There are three parts to this book. Part One extends pupils' understanding of important features of Muslim communities and the beliefs they express. Part Two focusses on Muslim family life. In Part Three pupils are helped to explore some of the ways in which individual Muslims apply their beliefs to their own personal lives. The three parts are indicated by colour coding: pink for Part One, blue for Part Two, yellow for Part Three. The coloured box round each page number shows which part the page is in.

Because this book is part of a structured and developmental scheme, some knowledge of Islam is assumed. However, some teachers may decide that a particular group of pupils does not have the assumed knowledge and is therefore not ready to proceed with this book. They may well decide that at least some preparatory work, using Book 1 in this set, is necessary.

Content overview of the pupils' books
The four pupils' books in this series are designed to help pupils develop an understanding of Islam as a world religion. Each book deals with different aspects of Islamic practices, beliefs and experiences.

The diagrammatic presentation below indicates the content of each book and shows how pupils are helped to build up, in a progressive way from 7–16, their knowledge and understanding of this religion. The shaded areas in the circles indicate the aspects of Islam dealt with in particular books.

A more detailed explanation of this way of distributing the subject matter across the four books is given in the teacher's books, **How do I teach R.E.?** and **Islam**.

MUSLIMS 1 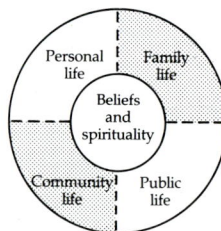 MUSLIMS 2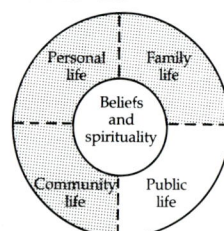

MUSLIMS 3 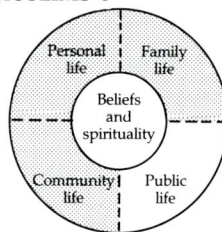 MUSLIMS 4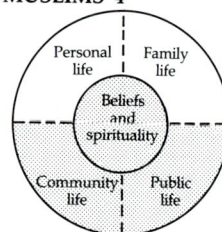

Other materials in this Project
Teachers using this book with upper primary pupils must realise that it is only one resource item designed to meet one specific aspect of the pupils' experience of R.E. – learning about Muslims. To expand the range of classroom activities designed to meet this need, a **photopack**, with additional pictures and information, is also available.

Teachers using these resources are strongly recommended to refer to the two teacher's books:
How do I teach R.E.? – the main Project manual.
Islam – a source book and guide to the teaching of this religion.

Books and photopacks relating to other religious traditions and various Life Themes are also part of **The Westhill Project R.E. 5–16.**